THE BOOK OF THE

SCHOOLS 4-4-0s

A Photographic Accompaniment

Notes by Richard Derry

IRWELL PRESS Ltd.

First published in the United Kingdom in 2006
by Irwell Press Limited, 59A, High Street, Clophill,
Bedfordshire MK45 4BE
Printed by Newnorth Print, Bedford

THE BOOK OF THE SCHOOLS 4-4-0s
A Photographic Accompaniment

Picture This

In the last few years we have seen the 'Book Of' series of locomotive studies develop into something of a library devoted to more and more of the principal BR express classes. Since 1997 there has been:

Beyond this a *de facto* journal has sprung up, in the shape of the *Photographic Accompaniments* to further celebrate these famous classes. These include, either published or projected:

Now it's the Schools' turn and once again the purpose is to serve up further photographs for a memorable class. Again, the idea is to accompany, supplement and complement the 'parent' volume, *The Book of the Schools 4-4-0s*. The Southern, like all four pre-Group companies, had a keen eye and ear for publicity and, like its rivals, was not above tweaking dimensions on a new design not for strictly engineering reasons but to get one over the opposition, statistically speaking. The all things to all men and largely meaningless 'tractive effort' came in particularly useful. Thus the Nelsons, briefly, could be claimed as the most powerful express engines in the country while the Schools (though here we are on much firmer ground) could be hailed as 'the most powerful locomotives of their type in the country'. This had the added merit of obscuring the fact that a 4-4-0 for top express work in 1930 could be portrayed, by those of an unkind mien, as something of a retrograde step.

The Schools were in essence a 'cross' in the breeding sense, a mix of Lord Nelson and King Arthur, though they avoided (spectacularly so) the frequent fate of such conjoinings. That they were so inherently effective right from the first discouraged endless sallies into that snare-strewn country signposted 'modifications'. Maunsell found no reason to amend his design, apart from a certain weakness which appeared in the bogie framing and even Bulleid largely steered clear of the 'V' class –

Something of a traditional posing place for new Maunsell locomotives, Charing Cross station and a beautiful brand new sage green E900 ETON. It has all the 'first features' an engine picker could count – original single sanding (to leading driver), the snazzy pointed smokebox door, lining even on the rear bogie wheel splasher, 'A' power classification on the running plate behind the buffer beam, snifting valves on the smokebox and so forth.

3

30900 ETON in BR days, entering Brighton station off the line from Hove and the west, with the Motive Power Depot in the background, 15 July 1958. The Bulleid carriages and headcodes indicate the Bournemouth train. ETON is very different now of course from the previous view, with deflectors and the big LeMaître exhaust, snifting valves long gone and the BR smokebox number plate obscuring the rakish 'point' behind it. Photograph Hamish Stevenson.

though he had less time than was the case with the Nelsons. Once he got his hands on the liveries though...

The true worth of the Lord Nelson 4-6-0s may lie in the way they 'enabled' the brilliant 'V' class, the Schools 4-4-0s. A Nelson engine, married to a King Arthur boiler and firebox, turned out to be a formidable locomotive. Maunsell had to come up with a markedly more powerful locomotive than the existing 4-4-0 post-Group L1 and its pre-Group sisters while matching some eye-wateringly tight loading/weight restrictions. LORD NELSON of 1926 had honed Maunsell's prodigious skills in designing increases in power with a minimal increase in its weight – the Nelson was a 'landmark' piece of work on a par with, say, the Princess Coronation Pacifics or the Britannias. And ETON wasn't far behind.

The Schools would succeed a variety of 4-4-0s though, as pointed out in the *Book Of*, nobody could have predicted that one day they would be tearing up and down on diagrams intended for Pacifics! With the boiler power of an Arthur and with the weight saving advantage of a whole coach, more or less, the Schools had a starting advantage that belied its looks. In the first design work the Nelson boiler was shortened for the Schools and a cylinder removed but further weight reduction was still necessary so a round top King Arthur type boiler/firebox replaced the

Nelson belpaire; it was the abandonment of this belpaire with its high shoulders (it would never have allowed enough room) that enabled the distinctively 'wrapped round' cab of the Schools. This made it eligible for the Hastings line, by accident, it could be said. The suitability of the Schools on this difficult route was thus a *by-product* of the design, not a fundamental part of it. The Schools came to be so closely associated with the highly restricted Hastings route but Maunsell never actually started out to design a locomotive for it.

Each Schools, where it was possible, was exhibited at the respective Public School after which it was named, or rather at the nearest convenient station. When others were named after schools remote from the Southern such as Harrow, Rugby and so on, there were no 'shows' The engines came out as follows:

March-October 1930
E900 ETON
E901 WINCHESTER
E902 WELLINGTON
E903 CHARTERHOUSE
E904 LANCING
E905 TONBRIDGE
E906 SHERBORNE
E907 DULWICH
E908 WESTMINSTER
E909 ST. PAUL'S

December 1932
910 MERCHANT TAYLORS

911 DOVER
912 DOWNSIDE
913 CHRIST'S HOSPITAL
914 EASTBOURNE

May-July 1933
915 BRIGHTON
916 WHITGIFT
917 ARDINGLY
918 HURSTPIERPOINT
919 HARROW

November-December 1933
920 RUGBY
921 SHREWSBURY
922 MARLBOROUGH
923 BRADFIELD (was Uppingham)
924 HAILEYBURY

May-August 1934
925 CHELTENHAM
926 REPTON
927 CLIFTON
928 STOWE
929 MALVERN

December 1934-August 1935:
930 RADLEY
931 KING'S WIMBLEDON
932 BLUNDELL'S
933 KING'S CANTERBURY
934 ST. LAWRENCE
935 SEVENOAKS
936 CRANLEIGH
937 EPSOM
938 ST OLAVE'S
939 LEATHERHEAD

The intricacies and intensity of

interest, even the occasional inanities that swirl around the devotion known as 'engine picking' so far as the Schools are concerned are of course fully exercised (or is it exorcised?) in *The Book of the Schools 4-4-0s*. These are complex and command much discussion in that very volume but a summary table or two will serve to activate the detail-spotting antennae of the average reader. Ensuring at the same time, we hope, that you buy the original book!

LIVERIES

Schools liveries were plain enough until Mr Bulleid tried his hand... The Table gives the dates of the main livery differences but there were a host of lining, numbering, lettering and detail, impossible to tabulate here.

Until plain black was adopted 'for the duration' in 1942 there were no less than *eight* combinations of livery/lining, and these are fully laid out in the 'parent' book.

The last to get plain wartime black was 934 in May 1945 but from the following year the fun began anew. First the wonderful

Table to show dates of principal alterations/events other than livery. The full 'engine picking' of the Schools is of course fully explored in the parent *Book of the Schools 4-4-0s*. These are complex and command much discussion in that very volume but a summary table or two will serve to activate the detail-spotting antennae of the average reader. Ensuring at the same time we hope, that you buy the original book too!

No.	'E' prefix removed	Flaman speed recorder	Lemaître Exhaust	Snifting valves removed	'S' prefix	BR No.	AWS	Speed-ometer	with-drawn
900	12/31	-	6/40	3/49	-	5/48*	-	1/60	2/62
901	1/32	-	10/40	9/48	-	10/48	6/60	6/60	12/62
902	11/31	-	-	2/50	-	1/49	4/59	-	12/62
903	11/31	10/38	-	1/47	-	3/48*	-	-	12/62
904	11/31	12/38	-	2/49	-	6/48*	-	-	7/61
905	7/31	11/38	-	8/49	-	9/49	-	11/60	12/61
906	10/32	4/39	-	11/49	-	12/49	5/62	11/60	12/62
907	12/31	9/39	11/40	6/48	-	8/48	-	12/59	9/61
908	9/31	11/38	-	5/49	-	3/49	6/59	-	9/61
909	1/32	9/39	2/41	9/47	-	1/49	-	12/60	1/62
910	-	-	-	11/48	-	12/48	6/60	-	11/61
911	-	-	-	7/49	-	8/49	-	10/60	12/62
912	-	-	-	2/49	-	3/49	5/60	5/60	11/62
913	-	-	-	6/48	-	9/48	6/59	-	1/62
914	-	1/39	1/39	2/48	3/48	5/50	4/59	-	7/61
915	-	-	10/40	8/47	-	2/49	8/60	8/60	12/62
916	-	-	-	9/48	-	11/48	-	12/59	12/62
917	-	5/39	5/40	3/48	-	5/48	8/59	-	11/62
918	-	10/38	5/40	8/46	-	10/49	4/59	-	10/61
919	-	10/38	2/41	11/49	-	8/48*	-	-	1/61
920	-	10/38	3/40	7/47	-	10/48	-	-	11/61
921	-	3/39	1/41	12/47	-	3/50	10/61	-	12/62
922	-	10/39	-	11/48	-	1/49	-	-	11/61
923	-	12/38	-	7/48	-	9/48	-	-	12/62
924	-	2/39	9/40	9/47	-	1/49	-	-	1/62
925	-	5/39	-	12/47	-	5/50	1/60	1/60	12/62
926	-	11/39	-	3/49	-	4/48*	10/60	10/60	12/62
927	-	-	-	10/49	-	11/49	5/60	11/59	1/62
928	-	9/39	-	5/48	-	6/48	7/59	-	11/62
929	-	6/39	3/41	7/47	-	1/49	8/61	1/60	12/62
930	-	-	4/40	6/48	-	7/48	4/60	4/60	12/62
931	-	11/38	7/39	2/48	-	10/48	-	1/60	9/61
932	-	-	-	6/48	-	7/48	-	-	1/61
933	-	12/38	5/40	4/48	-	6/48	-	-	11/61
934	-	-	5/40	1/48	2/48	9/48	5/62	2/60	12/62
935	-	-	-	11/48	-	12/48	6/59	5/60	12/62
936	-	-	-	7/48	-	7/48	11/59	11/59	12/62
937	-	-	5/39	12/47	-	9/48	9/60	9/60	12/62
938	-	-	6/40	1/49	2/48	3/49	-	3/60	7/61
939	-	A	8/40	5/47	-	4/48*	10/59	-	6/61

A Stone Deuta speedometer 8/38
* 6in. figures

An opportunity to see a Schools at work in the wartime black livery as 901 WINCHESTER heads a Hastings-London express in Hildenborough cutting. The date is not given but it is before the snifting valves were removed in 1948. The SR black was not as funereal as on some other lines, relieved as it was by the jaunty lettering.

malachite came back, though with sightly simplified lining and then came BR (LNWR) black. The BR of 1948, sadly, regarded a 4-4-0 as obsolescent and therefore unworthy of the dark (GWR) green. (A blessing in disguise some of us might humbly suggest.) We were then subjected to a further *six* combinations of lining, livery, numbering and lettering and again, these are set out in some very considerable detail in *The Book of the Schools 4-4-0s*. There's no way round it really, you've got to get the 'parent' book.

From July 1956 the BR (GWR) dark green with black and orange lining was adopted though four remained to the end in lined black – 30900, 30914, 30919 and 30932.

This *Accompaniment*, like the others, is designed as just that, to accompany and highlight and extend the coverage in the 'parent' *Book Of*. So, apart from very special thanks to Eric Youldon and Bryan Wilson, as well as Bob Ratcliffe and Norman Mundy, it's really straight to the pictures...

30901 WINCHESTER at Ashford shed, 4 October 1952. This species of BR black livery, lined in red, cream and grey, was the form which all forty Schools eventually enjoyed, though there were many variations in the first applications post-1948 before it settled down. Though 30901 (along with 30922, 30929 and 30937) had run for a time with the cab panel 'interrupted' by the framing, the 'uninterrupted' style shown here was the 'standard' form. Of all the various Schools liveries this was the only one to be borne by all the engines at the same time. That the Schools, despite their first rank work, got this mixed traffic garb, was owed to BR's official view that any 4-4-0 was obsolescent. In summary WINCHESTER's livery is: low cab lining, straight valence lining, 8in. number, small emblem, low tender lining, splashers lined. It had first been arrived at with 30900 in October 1950. Photograph B.K.B. Green, Initial Photographics.

No.	Sage Green*	Malachite Green	Olive Green	Wartime Black	Malachite Green	BR Black	BR Green
900	3/30	-	6/40	1/43	12/46	10/50	-
901	3/30	10/40	-	12/43	-	10/48	6/60
902	4/30	-	3/40	3/43	6/46	3/50	4/59
903	4/30	9/41	-	11/43	3/46	5/50	2/59
904	5/30	1/40	-	5/42	5/46	1/51	11/58
905	5/30	10/39	-	10/42	12/46	9/49	8/58
906	6/30	4/39	-	4/42	3/46	12/49	5/58
907	7/30	11/40	-	9/44	3/46	1/52	7/56
908	7/30	8/41	-	10/44	-	6/49	8/56
909	8/30	2/41	-	3/44	10/47	12/50	8/58
910	12/32	8/39	-	11/42	-	12/48	8/56
911	12/32	12/41	3/40	7/42	4/46	8/49	12/58
912	12/32	8/41	4/39	7/44	4/47	5/50	5/60
913	12/32	6/39	-	1/45	9/48	1/52	6/59
914	12/32	12/41	-	8/43	6/46	5/50	-
915	5/33	10/40	-	7/43	-	2/49	4/57
916	6/33	12/39	-	9/44	-	11/48	4/58
917	6/33	-	5/40	1/43	2/46	7/52	8/59
918	7/33	-	5/40	5/43	9/46	10/49	5/57
919	7/33	5/39	-	4/43	5/46	12/49	-
920	11/33	-	3/40	4/42	8/47	11/49	9/57
921	11/33	3/39	-	4/44	1/48	3/50	1/59
922	12/33	10/39	-	1/45	8/46	1/49	1/57
923	12/33	9/41	-	2/44	7/46	9/48	12/57
924	12/33	9/40	-	6/43	10/47	10/50	9/59
925	5/34	6/38	-	3/43	12/47	5/50	1/60
926	6/34	8/38	-	5/44	11/46	4/49	10/60
927	6/34	6/38§	2/40	9/43	8/47	11/49	3/58
928	6/34	7/38	-	4/42	6/48	12/50	7/59
929	8/34	6/38	-	1/44	-	1/49	12/56
930	12/34	6/38	-	10/42	7/48	3/50	10/56
931	1/35	7/40	-	12/42	-	10/48	10/58
932	2/35	7/38	-	8/45	7/48	2/51	-
933	3/35	5/40	-	10/43	6/48	6/51	6/58
934	3/35	3/41	-	5/45	1/46	1/50	2/60
935	6/35	5/39	-	9/43	-	12/48	12/56
936	6/35	7/39	-	5/44	9/46	3/49	11/59
937	7/35	4/39	-	12/45	9/48	12/50	1/57
938	7/35	2/39	-	1/44	3/46	3/49	10/56
939	8/35	8/40	-	3/43	4/48	10/50	3/57

Table of Schools liveries, from a broader one set out by D.W. Winkworth in *The Schools 4-4-0s* and subsequently amended in the light of later discoveries (personally communicated by Mr D.W. Winkworth and Mr E.S. Youldon, for which many thanks). First set out in *The Book Of The Schools 4-4-0s* (Irwell Press 2006).

* first livery – date is entry to traffic
§ Went to olive green (see next column entry) then reverted to malachite green 7/41
The precise month is often a matter of interpretation. How to determine 3/4/53 for instance? 3/53 or 4/53?
It may be useful, in view of the several published claims of it getting malachite green in 1946, to emphasise that 916 NEVER got malachite green post-war.

Awaiting its fate in Hove goods yard on 22 April 1963 with rods and name plates removed – these were the days before people bothered to nick number plates, obviously. The site accommodated a number of engines in this period – behind 30901 are two more Schools, an 0-6-2T and a couple of moguls, a K and a U1. Shadows reveal a second line up; in fact the full listing for Hove at this time was: Schools 30901, 30911, 30915, 30916. 30923, U1 31895, K 32338, 32341, 32342, E6 32417 and E4 32478. Photograph Peter Groom.

Simply perfect, E902 WELLINGTON in original condition. It still has the early form of bogie sideframe. This proved almost the only teething trouble on the Schools (it afflicted the Nelsons too) and was soon altered from this curved shape on the bottom edge to a straight form. Note how the lamp irons project out from the smokebox rim, as was the case with the Lord Nelsons. The route indicator discs, when on the irons, projected out to obscure the driver's vision, so they were moved to the smokebox door. Fitting deflectors meant they had to be moved to the smokebox door but this was done on 900-909 even before the deflectors appeared. There was originally a small handle (again, as with the Nelsons) on the right-hand side of the door (looking from the cab) which was removed to make way for the repositioned iron. Afterwards the smokebox door was opened by grasping the lamp iron on that side. The horizontal door handle was later shortened as on 30901 above.

A tired 30902 parked at the side of Basingstoke shed. It is late on, with the horrible livery of general grime. It had gone to Nine Elms at the end of 1960 (it might just have arrived, given the absence of shed plate) and 'the Basingstokes' from Waterloo and back were typical fare through to its withdrawal two years later. It's fairly pointless to comment on livery but we do have a good view of the AWS protector plate slung under the buffer beam. Photograph Paul Chancellor Collection.

Original sage green E903 CHARTERHOUSE with all original details, bogie, lamp irons, snifting valves, intricate lining to steps and just about everything else; sanding to leading driving wheels only.

A splendid 30903 CHARTERHOUSE on the 12.54pm to Basingstoke at Waterloo, 12 May 1959. It had got BR GW-style dark green ('belated green') a few months before. Lunch hour could usually be enlivened for photographer John Scrace by a Nine Elms Schools on the 12.54pm Waterloo-Basingstoke, a regular job for the class. They thus figure several times in these various pages. Photograph John Scrace.

E904 LANCING as built. Observe the delicacy of the motion; the fluted rods never required modification. It was this first ten, built in 1930, that emerged without the smoke deflectors which were already firmly established features of the Arthurs and Nelsons. There were smoke tunnel draughting experiments in progress at this stage so what to do with the new Schools was probably placed 'on hold'.

30904 LANCING at Tonbridge on 11 August 1954. It had been at St Leonards more or less from new but was finally wrenched from its seaside home with the Hastings diesel scheme of 1957. Photograph J. Robertson, The Transport Treasury.

30905 TONBRIDGE at Nine Elms shed, 16 May 1959. The tender, No.732, has an odd history. Originally with 932 BLUNDELL'S, in 1938 it was modified with higher sides so that the bunker was self-trimming, after the fashion of the Lord Nelsons. This was found to be unnecessary so no others were so dealt with. Twenty years later, a year or so before this view, it was painted green in error while 30932 was in black. In a case of 'shame to waste it' it was promptly put behind 30905, which was due to get green. And here it is. Strangely, while this extension looked good on a Nelson tender, it didn't seem quite right on a Schools. Photograph J.H. Aston.

30905 TONBRIDGE leaving Andover Junction with an excursion to Farnborough for the Air Show, 10 September 1961. Photograph S.C. Nash.

A Charing Cross-Hastings service behind 30906 SHERBORNE of St Leonards shed, climbing the 1 in 53/47 out of Tonbridge up to Somerhill Tunnel. The roof of Tonbridge engine shed and its coal stage can just be seen beyond the last coach on the curve. Photograph R.K. Collins, The Transport Treasury.

30906 SHERBORNE hurries along past Shalford at an unrecorded date. It got its speedometer (just visible) at the end of 1960 and hasn't yet got AWS (it was finally fitted in May 1962) which narrows the period down somewhat.

30907 DULWICH on a down passenger train at Sherborne, 10 July 1959. Photograph R.C. Riley, The Transport Treasury.

30908 WESTMINSTER, shed plate proclaiming one of its 73A Stewarts Lane periods (the third such, June 1957 to June 1959) with an up Ramsgate express at Gillingham, 30 September 1958. Photograph R.C. Riley, The Transport Treasury.

30908 WESTMINSTER in late condition with AWS but no speedometer (it never got one) at what looks to be Nine Elms. It had emerged from heavy repairs at Ashford in June 1959 equipped with AWS and went to the Western Section for the first time, to spend out its days at Basingstoke. It was thus 'up in London' much of the time. Slender footstep backplates on the tender denote a second-hand tender, used on a 4-6-0 prior to 1930. Photograph W. Hermiston, The Transport Treasury.

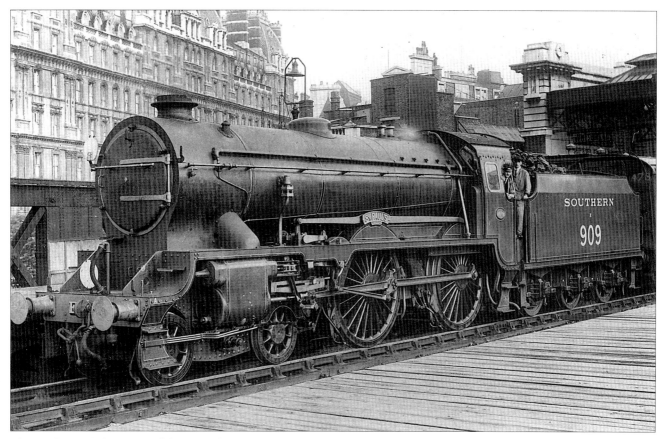

The traditional showcase of Charing Cross serves as usual for a perfect display, this time from new Schools E909 ST PAUL'S. As we leave the original batch of ten it's a good time to note one or two features, at the risk of repeating ourselves a little bit. We can marvel again at the intricate lining of the sage green livery, extending as it did to the steps and the bogie wheel splasher, the full contour of the running plate and so on. ST PAUL'S has all the original features, snifting valves, first type of bogie frame and so on but is noticeable for having sanding to *both* sets of driving wheels. I'm beginning to suspect that this last one of the batch, at least, emerged into traffic so equipped.

30910 MERCHANT TAYLORS on the 12.25pm Charing Cross-Hastings at London Bridge on 5 April 1949. Our Mr Aston photographed it twice on this occasion and a view in *The Book of the Schools 4-4-0s* shows it drawing away after a few minutes 'with a good smoke.' The loco had acquired BR black the year before. Photograph J.H. Aston.

30910 MERCHANT TAYLORS on the 5.5pm Cannon Street-Hastings near Grove Park, 11 May 1954. These are the north portals of Chislehurst Tunnel, known originally as 'Sunbridge Park Tunnel'. The original lines are the two on the right, the left-hand pair dating from the quadrupling from St Johns to Orpington, completed throughout in 1905. When the original tunnel was completed in 1865 a celebratory dinner for two hundred guests was held inside, with catering courtesy the London Bridge Refreshment Rooms. In 1902, while the quadrupling was under way, cracks were found in the original brickwork so the original line had to be closed for three months! Photograph R.C. Riley, The Transport Treasury.

30910 MERCHANT TAYLORS at its final home, Nine Elms, 30 April 1960. Photograph J.L. Stevenson, courtesy Hamish Stevenson.

30911 DOVER at Eastleigh shed, 30 August 1952. A Ramsgate engine, it was out that day from the works after a casual repair. Photograph R.J. Buckley, Initial Photographics.

30911 DOVER in the horrible BR grimy grey of the last years. It is a Redhill engine now, some time in 1962, before going to its final shed Brighton. It would be one of the Schools to languish in Hove goods yard after withdrawal. These are the Southern platforms at Reading; a Grange or a Hall is pointed in the Paddington direction in the distance. Photograph Paul Chancellor Collection.

The Schools came out in the standard SR 'Maunsell' or 'sage' green, with black and white lining and yellow lettering. They had oval numberplates on the cabside and tender rear and a prominent painted number on the tender side, which included a tiny 'E' (denoting Eastleigh as the maintaining works) until this was abandoned once the first ten had appeared. The first two, E900 and E901, had a block style on the buffer beam while the rest were serif. In place of the 'E' in the case of 902-909 and from the first in respect of the others, a 'No' with a dash and a point under the little 'o' was instituted, placed on the other side of the drawhook from the number. New cabside plates were cast. The tender lost its plate at the rear and the number was painted on instead. So 912 DOWNSIDE (in a frontal view at Charing Cross in June 1936 and side on at Cannon Street three months later) represents the original look of 'the rest', 910-939. The big change, however, was to the cab – from 910 onwards the cab window and the matching cab cut-out were increased in height by some six inches, because the original layout forced some crews to stoop uncomfortably when looking out. The increase left the strip between the top of the window/cut-out markedly narrower than before. The cabs of the first ten in fact look odd in comparison. Shorter smokebox handrail shown.

30912 DOWNSIDE with an up Margate express at Factory Junction, 26 May 1958. The junction got its name from the first 'factory' in the area, the LCDR Longhedge Works. From left to right are the Down Main, Up Fast and Up Slow of the LCD followed, on the right, by the Down South London and Up South London of the LBSCR. The station in the distance is Wandsworth Road which up until the Great War also had platforms on the LCD side. In 1958 this day (26 May) was Whit Monday so the normal 469 Turn (the 7.34am Margate-Charing Cross) would probably not have run. The train, it seems, was amended to cover this Margate-Victoria job which was, incidentally, a light Pacific duty! Photograph R.C. Riley, The Transport Treasury.

A new 913 CHRIST'S HOSPITAL on 'SPL 2' which would be a boat train. This is before the engine got malachite green in 1939, during the 1930s when it found itself backwards and forwards between St Leonards, Stewarts Lane and Ramsgate.

Resplendent in BR black, fresh out of Eastleigh in the winter of 1952. This was the last BR black livery 'category' – low cab lining, straight valence lining, 8in. number, small emblem, low tender lining, splashers lined – that became standard on all forty Schools. 30913 CHRIST'S HOSPITAL is so freshly assembled that the chalked ownership on the smoke deflectors ('913') is still quite clear – though it's now upside down. Photograph Lens of Sutton Collection.

Cannon Street on 30 May 1958 with 30913 CHRIST'S HOSPITAL leaving for Hastings. The signal box (its destruction by fire the previous year ushering in some months of emergency working) had stood on the left. Pacific 34025 WHIMPLE afterwards left with a Ramsgate train. Photograph R.C. Riley, The Transport Treasury.

914 EASTBOURNE was one of three or four Schools kept in especially tip-top condition and therefore used on specials on many occasions. So Eastbourne's very own EASTBOURNE was perfect for celebrating the seaside town's Jubilee Week in 1933. It served in this condition on the 'business train', the 9.30am up to Victoria; here it is on shed in its finery at Eastbourne, ready for the next working up to London. Photograph W.G. Boyden, Collection Frank Hornby.

30914 EASTBOURNE at Brighton shed, 20 July 1959. It has AWS, fitted a few months before, though it never got a speedometer. The engine is still in BR black and indeed was one of four that never got the BR green (the others were 30900, 30919 and 30932). In some instances (as here) clearly visible riveted/bolted plates were left on the smokebox when the snifting valves were removed. Photograph Hamish Stevenson.

Beautifully posed as usual at Charing Cross, a lovely sage green 915 BRIGHTON. The Schools were a blend, if you like, of Lord Nelson and King Arthur parts; Townroe (*The Arthurs, Nelsons and Schools of the Southern*, Ian Allan 1973) points to the amusing fact that Nelson front windows were used, turned upside down! BRIGHTON still has the original form of bogie frame with curved bottom edge. The loco was built with a plain top chimney, lost when it got a LeMaître exhaust in October 1940.

BRIGHTON now with the modified pattern of bogie frame. The slidebars look familiar – this Maunsell pattern (also used on the Nelsons) was adopted by Bulleid for his Pacifics. Square lined panel on cylinder. Photograph W. Hermiston, The Transport Treasury.

BRIGHTON at Brighton shed on the occasion of the 'Works Centenary Pullman Day', 5 October 1952. The Railway Correspondence and Travel Society organised its first Pullman specials (behind Brighton Atlantics) on 5 October and 19 October. For the visit to Brighton shed three engines associated with the name BRIGHTON were available, specially cleaned, for viewing – our very own Schools here along with A1X 0-6-0T 32640 and E5 0-6-2T 32587. Photograph J.H. Aston.

30915 BRIGHTON on the turntable at Newhaven shed, 21 August 1955. Trials in July 1948 showed that Schools could use the tightly curved shed yard and later in the year the 4-4-0s began to work Victoria-Newhaven boat trains. Photograph The Transport Treasury.

30916 WHITGIFT on an up train at Shortlands Junction, 27 July 1957. Shortlands sub-station is in the background. Here the two double lines from Herne Hill and the Catford Loop became a four track section eastward under the electrification scheme, avoiding many of the flat crossing delays. Hastings line coaches, some green, some crimson and cream. Photograph R.C. Riley, The Transport Treasury.

30916 WHITGIFT at St Mary Cray Junction, 14 June 1958. The new work is part of the Kent Coast Electrification (Phase 1) which authorised quadrupling from Bickley Junction to Swanley with the re-designing of the Chislehurst and Bickley Loops to raise speed from 30mph to 50mph. The new Up line is being prepared at the site where the new fast/slow double junction will be. The Chislehurst Loop can be seen beyond the end of the train, going off to the right. Compare with the view of 922 at the same location many years earlier (page 30) and the work nearing completion on page 53, with EPSOM. Photograph R.C. Riley, The Transport Treasury.

A beautifully new 917 ARDINGLY at Folkestone Junction in the 1930s with what would be a London train, worked up from the harbour by tank engines earlier on.

A deplorably scruffy 30917 ARDINGLY about 1950. She was a Ramsgate engine for 24 years. Only the trace of a panel on the smoke deflector indicates the malachite beneath, reapplied after the war, in 1946. This was the last Schools to lose malachite green, when it changed to BR black in July 1952. The Schools is on the Up Fast approaching Shortlands with an express for Margate. The view is from the bridge that links Kingswood Road with Queensmead Road east of Shortlands station. Photograph A.H. Lucas, The Transport Treasury.

Shortlands Junction again and 30917 heads an up express on 27 July 1957. Photograph R.C. Riley, The Transport Treasury.

918 HURSTPIERPOINT, in better condition than many of its fellows in this period, at Folkestone Junction on 25 April 1947. The engine is in the second malachite green, applied from the previous year. It is just possible to detect a trace of the deflector panelling. The first post-war malachite Schools had been 934 in January 1946, which had repeated the lining as applied before 1942. Not all got the second malachite and eight in the end passed directly from SR wartime black to lined BR black. Photograph H.C. Casserley, courtesy R.M. Casserley.

919 HARROW, in the original sage green livery, on a down express near Ashford in 1937.

Something of the 'pearl among swine' about HARROW in a view at the 'Old Shed' at Bricklayers Arms in the 1930s. The yard has yet to be cleared after the latest bout of firebox and smokebox cleaning. The primitive conditions only serve to highlight the exquisite lined sage green. You can follow the lining with your eye into almost every corner; and note the burnished safety valves! Photograph The Transport Treasury.

919 HARROW, unique in bearing Ashford's interpretation of malachite livery, namely black deflectors, green footsteps and green square panel on the cylinders. The location is Waterloo Eastern in 1947. HARROW retained this livery, apart from BR renumbering, until acquiring lined black in December 1949. Photograph F.G. Reynolds.

30919 HARROW at Stewarts Lane shed on 19 April 1958. It is in BR black; it never got green. So in HARROW we have a (very) potted history a Schools livery. Photograph J.L. Stevenson, courtesy Hamish Stevenson.

In a scene reminiscent of 30913 earlier on page 19 (in May 1958), 30920 RUGBY leaves Cannon Street for Hastings with the 5.5pm train, 5 June 1958. The Pacific this time is 34021 DARTMOOR. Photograph R.C. Riley, The Transport Treasury.

921 SHREWSBURY in post-War grime, at Tonbridge alongside that familiar and wonderful water column. The dirt in fact masks wartime black. As pointed out in *The Book of the Schools 4-4-0s*, it was sad but true that the plain black Schools were often in far better condition than the state they degenerated to come the 1960s. Photograph Collection Hamish Stevenson.

Now in lined BR black, 30921 SHREWSBURY at Stewarts Lane shed, 26 July 1951. It was one of the last to get its BR number, in March 1950.

30921 SHREWSBURY at Shortlands Junction on 2 August 1958 with 35015 ROTTERDAM LLOYD about to come beating past. The leading coach behind the Schools carries the boards: LONDON RAMSGATE BROADSTAIRS AND MARGATE. Photograph R.C. Riley, The Transport Treasury.

30921 SHREWSBURY at Nine Elms in final condition; AWS (but no speedometer) and reasonably clean given the time – and Lord Nelson tender. Two Schools, 30912 in June and 30921 in November 1961, got these high sided tenders. Apparently this was to increase the braking power available when working freight trains, though it hardly seemed worth the effort. You suspect they were hitched up more or less to avoid repairs to the Schools tenders then running. Photograph E.A. Elias, The Transport Treasury.

922 MARLBOROUGH with a down Victoria-Ramsgate train in the middle 1930s, at St Mary Cray Junction. It is the same location as 30916 on page 23 many years later, with the Kent Coast Electrification work going on.

Many sheds were closely associated with a particular type of express locomotive but none (probably) more completely than St Leonards and its Schools. The shed was a small place after all and the Schools stood out head and shoulders compared to other types. Restrictions ensured that no Pacifics or big 4-6-0s could ever overshadow them. 30922 MARLBOROUGH (note low-placed number) perfectly fits the 50ft turntable in August 1956. Photograph R.C. Riley, The Transport Treasury.

Malachite green 923 BRADFIELD (it had been UPPINGHAM until August 1934, a name which was removed at the insistence of the Headmaster) near Hildenborough in August 1947. 'Sir' had an absolute aversion to all forms of 'advertising'!

The Hove goods yard dump again, with 30923 nameless and abandoned. It has electrification flashes, which not all of them got, and has the bolted access panel on the cylinder casing, a feature which appeared late on. Photograph Peter Groom.

In malachite green in 1948 and in lovely condition apart from the strange blemish on the smoke deflector, 924 HAILEYBURY hurries along with a down Folkestone train at Chislehurst. It had lost the snifting valves the previous year and, note, the smokebox is plain without any patches...

30924 HAILEYBURY at Bricklayers Arms shed early in the 1950s now, however, with patches where the snifting valves had been! So smokebox, and probably boiler too, has been changed since the previous view. Photograph R.K. Collins, The Transport Treasury.

A year or two later out on the road at Chislehurst with a Charing Cross-Hastings train on 14 August 1954. Plain smokebox again! Photograph R.C. Riley, The Transport Treasury.

Immaculate in its new (first, pre-War) malachite, a polished 925 CHELTENHAM in 1938. Black smoke deflectors and extensive lining (the slightly more utilitarian post-War malachite did not generally include lining on the steps and the rear bogie wheel splasher).

A favourite for specials at the time, a glistening 30925 CHELTENHAM works a Royal Special past Wandsworth Road in 'the early 1950s'. The Royal Party, it is presumed, is bound for Epsom and the Races. Photograph Lens of Sutton Collection.

30925 CHELTENHAM at Cannon Street with an RCTS Special on 7 October 1962. A good view of how the cylinder drain pipes clipped neatly into a bracket on the front step. Photograph J.A.C. Kirke, The Transport Treasury.

30926 REPTON on, at a hesitant guess, the Dover turntable; it has the black livery of 1949 with blank tender (between 1948 and 1949 twelve Schools emerged in BR black but with tenders devoid of emblem). Snifting valves were removed at the same time, leaving in this instance a bolted circular plate. Ten inch number. Photograph W. Hermiston, The Transport Treasury.

REPTON was afterwards preserved in North America but has since returned. Here it is late in its BR life, while a Stewarts Lane engine 1961-1962. The plate covering the snifting valve opening on the smokebox has gone and the engine has acquired AWS, speedometer and green livery with second BR emblem on the tender.

927 CLIFTON in wartime black. Middle tender wheels are discs, outer pairs spoked! Photograph Collection Hamish Stevenson.

927 CLIFTON at Waterloo in 1938, shining bright in the new malachite just applied to the batch of Schools at Bournemouth. Alongside on pilot work is an M7 0-4-4T, No.40. O.J. Morris took a colour photograph on this occasion which *The Railway Magazine* proudly presented in its December 1938 issue.

928 STOWE was another of the Bournemouth Schools put in malachite green in 1938; here it is in the newly applied livery before the war, with an up train at Radipole Halt, August 1938. This would be a Dorchester crew, who took particular delight in 'opening up' the Schools at this time. Schools displaced by the Portsmouth electrification had migrated to Bournemouth (where they replaced 4-6-0s) in 1937 and in June and July 1938 six, including 928, got the new green, called Bournemouth green at first because the stock was similarly painted. This was 'malachite' and 928 was fairly unusual in having plain black cylinders. They worked, among much else, the morning up and afternoon down 'Bournemouth Limited' to and from Weymouth, though here STOWE is on the 5.37pm Weymouth-Waterloo which was not named.

30928 STOWE with a Hastings-Charing Cross train on 19 April 1958. This is Somerhill tunnel, south of Tonbridge. Photograph R.C. Riley, The Transport Treasury.

Atmospherically charged portrait at Ashford (being rebuilt for the first time, in 1960-61) with 30928. STOWE bears AWS, electrification flashes and the panel over the cylinder covers; third rail has appeared but electric working didn't commence till January 1961. STOWE was withdrawn from Brighton in December the following year. The signal gantry is a temporary one; bridge widening required the removal of an older bridge at this end and, along with it, the platform end signals. The gantry in turn was removed upon the Ashford resignalling of April 1962. Photograph The Transport Treasury.

929 MALVERN, another of the Bournemouth Schools put into malachite in that summer of 1938. The engine could be almost in 'royal' condition.

30929 MALVERN near Bickley Junction, 14 August 1954. A summer Saturday in the school holidays, a footpath and a wire fence were all the trainspotting ingredients we needed. Photograph R.C. Riley, The Transport Treasury.

Southern Railway " Schools " Class 4-4-0 Express Passenger Locomotive.

Postcard Schools. 930 RADLEY issued in the cause of SR publicity. It is incorrectly described on the reverse as 'E 930'. Nice to trip someone else up for a change! Modellers note: tender corner cutaway was deeper at the front than at the back on a Schools.

930 RADLEY at Portsmouth Harbour, 22 May 1937. It was a local engine, one of the Fratton complement but would soon go to Bournemouth, getting the malachite the following year. Photograph H.C. Casserley, courtesy R.M. Casserley.

931 KING'S WIMBLEDON fairly new and luxuriating in the sage
green livery (with panelled cylinder) in the shed yard at Nine Elms.
It would be ready to work back to Portsmouth and its home shed,
Fratton. A good view of the sanding arrangements and all the gear
below the running plate, including the relatively delicate fluted rods
and the form of balance weight applied to a handful of Schools when
a reduced degree of balancing was tried.

30931 KING'S WIMBLEDON passing Ashford with an up express, 20 April 1957. Photograph B.W.L. Brooksbank, Initial Photographics.

Now in BR green, KING'S WIMBLEDON takes a more modest load up the 1 in 100 gradient through Orlestone Woods, after leaving Ham Street & Orlestone with the Sunday 6.50am Hastings-Ashford train. Photograph Dennis Ovenden.

932 BLUNDELL'S newly garbed in glorious malachite, at Waterloo in the summer of 1938. Newly attached is the high Lord Nelson style tender, No.732; the Schools did not suffer from the problem of coal failing to work forward while running so it was unnecessary and was not repeated. This was the tender of course that was painted green in error in 1958 (see earlier) while BLUNDELL'S itself was getting another coat of black. Rather than paint it back again it was transferred to 30905, then in the process of becoming green. 30932 BLUNDELL'S, to teach it a lesson, remained black to the end.

BLUNDELL'S in black, unfortunately with Lord Nelson style tender obscured in the dark confines of the 'Old Shed' at Bricklayers Arms, 25 April 1953. Photograph A.R. Carpenter, The Transport Treasury.

933 KING'S CANTERBURY in scintillating sage green livery, black deflectors, exquisite lining and so on. It was hardly in better condition when turned out for Derby Day 'royals' some twenty years later. It is thought to be working a Birkenhead-Bournemouth through train in 1939 (Maunsell set 459 was dedicated to this working) and the location is believed to be between Reading West and Basingstoke. It had presumably taken over the working at Oxford and would have come round the Reading West Curve. Photograph M.W. Earley.

30933 KING'S CANTERBURY with an up Ramsgate express at Bickley Junction, 30 September 1958 with Kent Coast Electrification (Phase 1) work underway. Photograph R.C. Riley, The Transport Treasury.

30933 KING'S CANTERBURY at Folkestone Central, 4 August 1957. The fabled rivet counters will have noted by now that Schools buffer beams started off plain and generally got more complicated, as here. Though some didn't... Photograph J. Robertson, The Transport Treasury.

The usual mystifying goings-on at Kensington Olympia with 30934 ST LAWRENCE and a Type 2 (D5017 also off the Southern and failed, incidentally) on 6 August 1960. The SR Fireman is checking the connections behind the Schools, its LM articulated stock forming the 11.5am Margate-Kidsgrove. The 4-4-0 would hand over to an LM loco at Mitre Bridge. Once again we have the strange survival of the 74A shedplate: the Ashford '74' District had disappeared a couple of years before; 30934, indeed, had gone there *after* 74A had theoretically become 73F! Things are never quite what they seem... Photograph R.C. Riley, The Transport Treasury.

30934 ST LAWRENCE in BR black, at Sevenoaks on 30 March 1957 with the 11.10am Hastings-Charing Cross. Photograph Frank Hornby.

As intimated earlier the Schools buffer beams form fertile ground for the Rivet Counter. Their look changed over time though not particularly consistently from one engine to the next. From more or less flush with a few rivet heads at the outer sloping ends, horizontal and vertical rows of rivet heads appeared. With AWS came the arrangement shown here, on 30934 ST LAWRENCE sadly withdrawn and awaiting scrapping at Eastleigh, 2 June 1963. Two vertical brackets were associated with the AWS, plus conduit and protective shield below the buffer beam, though some got AWS while still retaining a (relatively) flush buffer beam. ST LAWRENCE peculiarly, and as described in *The Book of the Schools 4-4-0s*, spent a lengthy time out of use after withdrawal but, remarkably, had been put into steam in May 1963 a full five months after withdrawal in order to haul an 0-6-0 (30368 according to Bradley) from Basingstoke to Eastleigh, where the pair were eventually cut up. It was thus, by strange chance, the last Schools to be in service in steam. Photograph The Transport Treasury.

A sage green 935 SEVENOAKS, snifting valves and church spire prominent.

30935 SEVENOAKS with that familiar backdrop, the 'Old Shed' at Bricklayers Arms, 2 April 1955. Photograph A.R. Carpenter, The Transport Treasury.

30935 SEVENOAKS, believed to be at Weymouth, which makes it an unusual picture for a Schools but look at that shed code. It is clearly late, the 1960s, and new electrification flashes have appeared. By rights the period of this picture should be 1962 when the engine *should* be carrying the 70A of Nine Elms, let alone the non-existent 73F of Ashford...

A Royal race day train, behind 30936 CRANLEIGH, Oaks Day 1954. The Oaks, for fillies only, was then run on the Friday after the Derby. The engine is beautifully cleaned in the noble BR black but the extra highlighting to the wheel rims, smokebox door straps, deflector rims and so on is not necessarily pleasing to all – an unnatural prancing circus horse look, as expounded in *The Book of the Schools 4-4-0s*! Photograph Ted's Dad.

Denmark Hill, and 30936 CRANLEIGH heads a down Ramsgate train, 16 May 1959. Photograph R.C. Riley, The Transport Treasury.

937 EPSOM in 1939 with modified cylinders, exhaust, vast rimless chimney and extended smokebox; this led to some notable performances but it eventually reverted to the standard arrangement...

...as here. 30937 heads a down train at Sydenham Hill, 30 March 1959. Photograph R.C. Riley, The Transport Treasury.

30937 EPSOM with the 1.20pm Victoria-Ramsgate at St Mary Cray Junction, 16 May 1959. The new work of the Kent Coast Electrification (Phase 1) has moved on from the view of WHITGIFT in June 1958 on page 23. Photograph R.C. Riley, The Transport Treasury.

938 ST OLAVE'S, as new in sage green. It was a Bricklayers Arms engine and remained so virtually for its entire working life.

Two views of new 939 LEATHERHEAD out on the road. The Schools tenders were small (though agreeable on the eye) and on a system without troughs, 4,000 gallons was about the practical minimum on express workings. On other classes 5,000 gallons and more became 'the norm'.

Perfect pairing, at what looks like Shorncliffe outside Folkestone. 30938 ST OLAVE'S is overtaken by light Pacific 34075 264 SQUADRON. It would be about 1949-50, with the Schools newly in BR black and the Battle of Britain with the early BR buffer beam number plus number plate.

Finale. 30939 LEATHERHEAD amid fellows at Stewarts Lane shed, 10 May 1959. Bolting of chimney to smokebox clearly shown. Photograph R.C. Riley, The Transport Treasury.

THE BLACK BOX... THE BLACK BLACK BOX...

Regretfully errors creep in to these volumes; very rarely (it is a relief to report) do they concern the locomotive details but rather they are idiotic typographical slip-ups which seem impossible to completely hunt down and destroy, calamities such as the wrong image selected at the last minute (publisher: note) or they concern the locations. Now one, of course, happily and manfully shoulders the blame for any error, though undated anonymous fields and woods, while perfectly bloody obvious to some of us, will mean an element of detective work for the rest of us. So here we go...

In *The Book of the Schools 4-4-0s* where better to start than page 1? The reference to top-hatted boys should read page 26, not page 36. Under 'Contents', page 25 should read 15! On page 23 30925 is of course at London Bridge not Cannon Street. Similarly on page 109 the train is leaving Charing Cross, not Cannon Street. On page 65 a typing error saw 30913 heading the 12.45pm to Basingstoke when it was in fact the 12.54pm. 'All the Basey semi-fasts' writes Jim Aston, 'in the off-peak were 0.54, changed to 0.09 and 0.39 in the peaks'. On page 127 'Folkestone to the coast' plainly was meant to read *on* the coast. Dave Pulham also remarked on this geographical impossibility. On page 28 the wording 'looks like 455' obviously should be 'looks like 466'.

Eric Youldon writes: 'Photographs have surfaced that make the note in the March 1961 *Railway Observer* and quoted on page 4 of *The Book of the Schools 4-4-0s* incorrect. 30936 was definitely *not* changed to green in April 1961; it had run in this livery since November 1959 when ex-works after a general overhaul. The 1961 visit was for a light casual only thus making 30926 the last Schools to be repainted BR green from black, in October 1960. Unfortunately the errant date crops up several time so correction is called for as follows:

Page 4: 30936 was thus not the last green one.

Page 20: In the table 936 should change from 4/61 to 11/59.

Page 21: '30936 in April 1961' to read '30926 in October 1960' in column one.

Page 121: In the penultimate works visit, add BR Green and delete BR Green in the final entry.

'That 1961 RO has a lot to answer for I'm sorry to say because as there was no correction subsequently, authors have ever since innocently listed the wrong date for 30936 into BR Green.

'30928 also has to come under the spotlight. The date for its entering service in BR black was 12/50 and *not* 6/49 which has been consistently reported for years. Photographs now to light indicate this is wrong. 'The Book Of' therefore requires correcting thus:

Page 20: In the BR Black column of the Table, 928 should read 12/50 instead of 6/49.

Page 21: In column one remove 30928 from the 3/49-9/49 group and place it in the 5/50-10/50 group.

Page 101: In the Works table, BR Black should be in the next line, so that it follows "86,283".'

At places like Blackpool, rows of locomotives parked alongside seaside facilities didn't seem to bother anyone but on the south coast particularly with the white fronted houses, not to mention the washing, they didn't quite fit. A Sunday at St Leonards shed, 5 July 1953, finds an impressive 30903 CHARTERHOUSE in such surroundings. Photograph B.K.B. Green, Initial Photographics.